GETTING TO KNOW
THE U.S. PRESIDENTS

GERALD R.
FORD

THIRTY-EIGHTH PRESIDENT
1974 – 1977

WRITTEN AND ILLUSTRATED BY MIKE VENEZIA

CHILDREN'S PRESS
AN IMPRINT OF SCHOLASTIC INC.
NEW YORK TORONTO LONDON AUCKLAND SYDNEY
MEXICO CITY NEW DELHI HONG KONG
DANBURY, CONNECTICUT

Reading Consultant: Nanci R. Vargus, Ed.D., Assistant Professor, School of Education, University of Indianapolis

Historical Consultant: Marc J. Selverstone, Ph.D., Assistant Professor, Miller Center of Public Affairs, University of Virginia

Photographs © 2008: AP Images: 12, 30; Corbis Images: 5, 29, 31 (Bettmann), 22, 28 (Wally McNamee); Courtesy of Gerald R. Ford Presidential Library: 13 (reprinted with permission of Cosmopolitan Magazine), 3, 7, 9, 15, 17, 18, 20, 21, 23, 27; Getty Images/Ian Wagreich: 32.

Colorist for illustrations: Andrew Day

Library of Congress Cataloging-in-Publication Data

Venezia, Mike.
  Gerald R. Ford / written and illustrated by Mike Venezia.
    p. cm. — (Getting to know the U.S. presidents)
  ISBN-13: 978-0-516-22642-2 (lib.bdg.)   978-0-516-25597-2 (pbk.)
  ISBN-10: 0-516-22642-8 (lib. bdg.)   0-516-25597-5 (pbk.)
  1. Ford, Gerald R., 1913–Juvenile literature. 2. Presidents—United
States—Biography—Juvenile literature. I. Title.
  E866.V46 2008
  973.925092—dc22
  [B]
                                      2006102930

1 2 3 4 5 6 7 8 9 10 R 17 16 15 14 13 12 11 10 09 08

President Gerald R. Ford in the Oval Office with his dog, Liberty

Gerald Ford was the thirty-eighth president of the United States. He was born on July 14, 1913, in Omaha, Nebraska. Gerald Ford became president when Richard Nixon suddenly resigned. President Ford's good nature and honesty were just what the country needed at the time.

While Richard Nixon was president, he was involved in some sneaky, illegal activities. At first, the president denied it. Soon, however, it was discovered that Nixon had approved of wiretapping and burglarizing his opponents' offices to gather information about them.

President Nixon then tried to hide evidence that would prove his guilt. Rather than face a trial and be forced to lose his important job, Richard Nixon decided to resign on August 8, 1974. The next day, Vice President Gerald Ford was sworn in as the next president of the United States.

President Nixon left the White House by helicopter on August 9, 1974, the day after he resigned as president.

Jerry Ford got off to a very confusing start in life. Jerry's father's name was Leslie Lynch King. When Jerry was born, he was named Leslie Lynch King, Jr. When Jerry was three, his parents got divorced.

His mother remarried, and Jerry took the name of his new father, Gerald Rudolf Ford, Sr. Jerry was OK with his new name. He respected and loved his new dad very much.

Gerald Ford at age fourteen (second from left) with his stepfather and his three half brothers.

Jerry grew up in Grand Rapids, Michigan. When he started school, teachers discovered he was ambidextrous, which means he was both right-handed and left-handed. Jerry would use his right hand when he stood up and his left hand when he was sitting!

Gerald Ford (holding flag) as an Eagle Scout at age sixteen

Jerry's parents taught him and his three half-brothers the importance of being honest and working hard. These qualities helped Jerry achieve the highest honor in the Boy Scouts, becoming an Eagle Scout.

Jerry Ford did well in high school and college. He really stood out, though, for his athletic ability. Jerry helped both his high-school and college football teams to win championships.

There were other presidents who were good at sports. Abe Lincoln was known for his wrestling ability. Teddy Roosevelt was a boxer and member of his college rowing team. Dwight D. Eisenhower was a football hero while in school. But Jerry Ford was the only

president who had offers to play professional sports. Both the Detroit Lions and Green Bay Packers offered Jerry contracts. If there had ever been a Presidential Football League, Jerry Ford's team would most certainly have been the league champs.

Jerry Ford was a star football player at the University of Michigan.

Jerry decided against playing professional football. Instead, he continued his education. After graduating from the University of Michigan, Jerry attended Yale University in Connecticut. At Yale, Jerry worked as an assistant football and boxing coach while he studied law.

The good-looking Jerry Ford also made extra money by modeling. He and his girlfriend even modeled for the covers of some national magazines!

Ford served as the model for this 1942 magazine cover.

After getting his law degree at Yale, Jerry started a law business in Grand Rapids. Just a few months later, the United States entered World War II. Jerry decided to join the U.S. Navy. During the war, Jerry's ship was involved in all kinds of battles. But Jerry's closest brush with danger actually happened back in the United States. While flying between air bases,

Jerry's plane had to make a crash landing. Everyone just barely escaped before the plane exploded in flames.

When the war ended, Jerry got back to his law business. Around this time, he was introduced to a young woman named Betty Bloomer. Betty worked at a local department store as a fashion-display designer. She was also a model and an accomplished dancer. Jerry and Betty hit it off right away. After dating for a while, they decided to get married.

Betty Bloomer practicing a dance routine in 1938

It was a busy time for Jerry Ford. While he was getting ready to marry Betty, he also decided to run for Congress. While in the navy, Jerry had formed some strong opinions about making life better in the United States. During this time, many people in Michigan, including Jerry's opponent, Bartel "Barney" Jonkman, were isolationists.

Jerry Ford talks to farmers while running for Congress in 1948.

This meant they thought the United States was better off if it minded its own business and didn't get involved in the world's problems. Jerry felt the opposite. He believed the United States had to work with and help out other nations. Jerry wanted the United States to remain a world leader in order to stay free and avoid future wars.

The 1948 Ford campaign headquarters were in an army surplus building called a Quonset hut.

Jerry was a member of the Michigan Republican Party. He campaigned hard to convince the voters of his district that he would be the best man to represent them in Congress. Jerry first won an early election, called a primary, against his Republican opponent.

He then won the general election against the Democratic candidate. Gerald Ford became a member of the U.S. House of Representatives in 1949. He was working so hard on the election, he barely had time to think about getting married.

Congressman Gerald Ford, in front of the Capitol building in Washington, D.C., puts a Michigan license plate on the back of his car in 1955.

Jerry Ford had a great career representing the people of his state. He was reelected twelve times. Jerry even became the leader of the Republican Party in the U.S. House of Representatives. He was well liked by both Republicans and Democrats.

Jerry and Betty ended up having three sons and a daughter. They often traveled between their home near Washington, D.C., and one in Grand Rapids, Michigan.

Jerry Ford, his wife Betty, and their four children at their home near Washington, D.C., in 1958

After spending twenty-four years in Congress, Jerry Ford began to think about retiring from politics. Then something happened that would change his life forever. In 1973, President Nixon's vice president, Spiro T. Agnew, was found guilty of receiving illegal bribes when he was the governor of the State of Maryland.

Vice President Spiro Agnew resigned in 1973.

President Richard Nixon (second from left) meets in the Oval Office with (from left to right) Secretary of State Henry Kissinger, Vice President Gerald Ford, and Chief of Staff Alexander Haig.

Agnew was forced to resign. President Nixon had to find a new vice president right away. He needed someone who was upright, honest, and trustworthy. President Nixon chose Gerald Ford.

If it wasn't bad enough having Spiro Agnew resign in disgrace, President Nixon began having his own big-time problems. Investigators and news reporters were beginning to find evidence that the president had approved of spying on his Democratic opponents.

The spying had taken place at the Watergate Hotel and office complex. This was where the Democrats had their campaign headquarters. The whole mess became known as the Watergate scandal.

At first, President Nixon denied having anything to do with any illegal activities. Because Jerry Ford was always honest, he expected other politicians to be honest, too. Gerald Ford believed President Nixon, and spent lots of time defending his boss.

It didn't take long, though, before Vice President Ford realized Richard Nixon and his friends might not be telling the truth. Soon there was talk of President Nixon possibly leaving his job in order to avoid being tried for illegal activities.

Gerald R. Ford is sworn in as the thirty-eighth president of the United States on August 9, 1974.

Vice President Ford's supporters thought it might be a good idea to start getting ready in case Ford was asked to take over the country's top job. In August 1974, Richard Nixon resigned. Without ever being voted into office, Gerald Ford became the next president of the United States.

After the Watergate scandal, the country's trust in its government was at an all-time low. President Ford's natural friendliness and open honesty helped show the nation it was once again in good hands.

Jerry Ford's two-and-a-half years as president were packed full of activity. He worked hard to get the Soviet Union to limit its testing of nuclear weapons.

President Ford with Soviet Premier Leonid Brezhnev

In 1975, Communist forces in Cambodia seized the U.S. ship *Mayaguez*, which carried a crew of thirty-nine men. President Ford sent in the Marines to rescue the crew. The mission was accomplished, but the cost was high. Forty U.S. soldiers were killed in the rescue operation.

He did his best to improve the nation's economic problems. In 1975, an American cargo ship, the *Mayaguez*, was captured by Communist forces in Cambodia, a country in Asia. President Ford sent U.S. marines in to rescue the crew. His quick action showed the world that the United States would never stand for being pushed around by anyone.

President Ford ducks behind his limousine after a shot is fired at him as he leaves a hotel in San Francisco on September 22, 1975.

Two different people tried to assassinate Gerald Ford. Luckily, both times, the president escaped unharmed, and both times, the would-be assassins were captured right away. President Ford probably received the most attention, though, for giving Richard Nixon a full pardon for any crimes he may have committed.

The president wanted to put the embarrassing Watergate scandal in the past and help the country heal by moving on. Jerry Ford truly believed he did the right thing. He was surprised when people became angry. Many citizens wanted Richard Nixon to face charges and be tried for his crimes.

One month after Richard Nixon's resignation, President Ford signs Nixon's pardon.

In 1999, President Bill Clinton presented Gerald Ford with the Presidential Medal of Freedom, the United States' highest civilian honor.

Gerald Ford ran for a second term, but he didn't win. Too many people were upset with him for pardoning Nixon. Even though Gerald Ford was trustworthy, people wanted a president who had no connection to Richard Nixon.

Jerry and Betty moved to California. Jerry kept busy writing books, setting up the Gerald Ford Library in Ann Arbor, Michigan, and playing golf. He received the Presidential Medal of Freedom in 1999 for the good work he did as president. Gerald Ford lived to the ripe old age of ninety-three. He died peacefully at home on December 26, 2006.